IT GROWS IN WINTER

IT GROWS IN WINTER
AND OTHER POEMS

CHINYERE GRACE OKAFOR

Africa World Press, Inc.

P.O. Box 1892 P.O. Box 48
Trenton, NJ 08607 Asmara, ERITREA

Africa World Press, Inc.

P.O. Box 1892

Trenton, NJ 08607

P.O. Box 48

Asmara, ERITREA

Copyright © 2008 Chinyere Grace Okafor

Book design: Aliya Books
Book cover: Ashraful Haque

Library of Congress Cataloging-in-Publication Data

Okafor, Chinyere Grace.
It grows in winter and other poems / Chinyere Okafor.
   p. cm.
ISBN 1-59221-586-6 -- ISBN 1-59221-587-4 (pbk.)
I. Title.

PR9387.9.O3747I8 2007
821'.914--dc22

                    2007024169

Contents

Dedication

In memory of our brother,
Augustine Aniamalu Esom:

This unacknowledged artist,
who cheered the artist in me,
Made an exit from our canvas,
but in our hearts he lives —
His stories, music, and drawings.

Description by the author

Many of the poems derive from the beauty and happiness in Nigeria and the conflicted situations where communities are overwhelmed by disasters, strikes, and riots, as well as international locales and situations that are equally challenging. While my plays such as *Campus Palaver, The Lion and The Iroko*, and *The New Toyi Toyi* engage solutions through public stage scrutiny, poetry offers me private respite for inquiry.

The persona engages loved ones such as family and friends, as well as adversaries such as war, death, apartheid, ethnic cleansing, and terror. Although frustrations may appear like curses as in "Khaki Throne" and "When I Get Your Heart," they are mostly subversive and celebrative of the essences that empower resilience. "Laughter" and the poetic journey are partners as much as the muse and the persona are one in the struggle.

The world is so endowed with beauty and richness that hunger and devastation are incongruous. Why do people kill other people? Why my country? Why me? Why? These are some of the questions that underlie this writing. We cannot resign to the idea that *Ujiri di uto na anyi ido* (The apple that is delicious frolics with soldier ants), but must fight the 'ants' and restore the dignity of life.

The heroine's strength and faith grow in the battle with winter which, although a challenger, is turned to ally just like real-life winter in Kansas, Maine, and Swaziland. It is through suffering that we grow tough, that we become whole. The strong one can account for every wrinkle; every grey hair that marks a point of great effort and so improves the beauty of the human being.

Inspiration Pest

"When we sleep is our night.
When we wake is our morn."
Says the spirit that calls the tune,
In my dance of death and birth.

My dance defies control.

From seven to seven,
It searches and lashes,
It dishes and trashes,
Like a tireless lover,
Seeking a goal.

My dance defies control.

Sometimes it hangs in the air,
And pushes pots of poetry,
In different different shapes.
I have no choice but keep the date,
For I am at the mercy of this restless muse.
. . .
And so,
The first seven and all the rest,
Come in heat of dance, unguided by pause:

My Love Grows in Winter

My love for you grows in winter,
When the grass turns brown,
And birds return to their nests.
My love for you feeds on shrubs.
It eats the thin leaves of winter.

The hills that litter your waist,
Are seen in the sundry curves,
And colors of Swazi fields,
Laid bare by the winter winds.

I gaze at the darkening meadows,
I fear and wonder how your love is.

Is it cold like winter biting my body?
Is it making fire in the chill of distance?

Do not echo my fear, that you call me deserter;
Heartless one who left, in harmattan of our life.

Not so, dear land, I am no deserter.
I am still your own clinging to you,
And claiming your love so scarce,
In this harmattan of your life.

I shall still come to you,
Even in your battered shape,
Disfigured by strife and all that came in the new harmattan.

I shall come smelling of fondness and shining of distance;
You will have no choice but to forgive my brief desertion.

Surely my love grows in winter for my battered homeland.

(Published in *TurfWrite: A Creative Writing Journal*, 1999)

Breath of Mother Earth

Did you see the hills of Aro-of-God,
Rising like shackled mounds,
From the chest of Mother Earth?

Did you caress their cheeks,
With breath of Mother Earth,
Carried in your bowels,
As you swept the hills of my homeland?

Did you breathe on my loved ones?
Did they smell me in your breath?
Did they know that you brushed me?
Did they feel me? Did . . did . . did they-?

Please, next time you glide across my home,
Remember to spray greetings in the yard,
With leaves that richly garnish the valleys.

Remember to whisper my love,
Through the palm trees of my home,
For my people drink the love of the palm.

Thank you for acceding to my plea.
Thank you for this grand connection.
Thank you, Breath of Mother Earth.

Winter Love

My winter love is no winter,
But summer covered in snow.
It is fall color masked by need.

My love for you is no winter.
It is not scarce like my song,
Subdued by the cold.

My longing for you rises,
Like Nsukka hills in the fog,
With clouds that mask ascent.

Hide and seek are my belly buttons.
Even my heart has legs that jump,
As longing wraps you in mirages,
Hides the green hills of my love.

You will see when the snow melts,
How I will swell with your love.

Loneliness

Straining my neck for chances,
Of sniffing another traveler,
Manzini Street throws lances,
At this lonely wayfarer,
In search of deserted folks.

Empty halls tell tales,
Of happy times.
Empty roads now hail,
The heavy signs,
Of lively crowds and busy sales.
Even a drum, abandoned,
Tells its own former tales.

My ears stare at spaces.
My soul swims in tears.
My sob sounds a false note,
In this sorrowful song.

January 22, 1996

(On entering Manzini during the general strike of people
against the State)

Nostalgia

Nostalgia gnaws at me.
It crawls down,
Chokes my throat,
Balloons,
The tips,
My heart soaks with blood!
Oh my God.
I run.

Withered bitterleaf hedge!
Winter slaps me with vice.
Arrest!

Oh, this pest.

Gazing at Wide Country

Relocation to Kansas jamed stiff reaction:
"It's jus flat," from Tae Kwon Do teacher.
I thought that he meant my *hun jin*.
My partner broke the protocol of discipline:
"There's nothing there 'cept corn fields," he jabbed.
"No ocean or lakes, just heat and sun," another jab.
Their reaction killed my concentration.
Needless to say; I lost the fight.

The exercise and discipline of Tae Kwon Do always erased the
tensions and irritations of my daily life as a black foreign
woman. This was why I attended the class. Religiously.

Earlier that day, I wanted to borrow a video for my class. I
introduced myself as an instructor and gave the officer my card.
She said that she could not help, because only instructors were
allowed to borrow videos. Didn't she hear my introduction or
see my designation on the card?

 "I'll handle it. She's Faculty," The manager intervened.
"She doesn't look like an instructor," The officer maintained.
"What does an instructor look like?" My mouth and eyes
queried.
"Oh. I don't really know, I guess." Her mouth countered.
"You don't have the guts to say it," I said, in my heart.
"I'm not socially allowed to say it." She might have said, in her
heart.

The manager smiled at me. I smiled also.
The pretense of political correctness.
We both knew the thing that was not said.

Unsaid things, and all the pretence,
Irritate me more than the said things.

I carried irritation in my heart,
But it pulled down my shoulders,
And drew lines on my face.
So, I girded myself for:

Tae Kwon Do

Tae Kwon Do wrestles my spirit.
It combs this body with punches.
Tae Kwon Do fixes frustrations.

"All hope is lost, when Tae-Kwon-Do causes frustration." This
was what I thought as my Tae-Kwon-Do teacher and colleagues
bombarded me with negative thoughts about my relocation to
Kansas. That day, I left the gym with shoulders that sank into a
heart that was empty, for not only did they kill my concentra-
tion, they also piled me with extra weight.

I turned to Mother, but cosmic elements cut our dialogue.
So, I recalled the words that she had fed my ears:
"Stand firm on the ground. Listen to your heart.
Connect with earth, the sky, and all in-between."
This led me to Wichita, Kansas, to the garden of inspiration
where I felt wide country:

Wide Country

Wide country that stretches my eyes to the domain of memory,
Where landscape of imagination is watered by contemplation.
You salute my body with hefty winds,
You assault me with crowds of wind,
That wrestle my path,
As I jog by the lakes of Rock Road.

Wide country that washes eyes with waves of acclimatization.
Rain, hail, sun and all that fight for space and wrestle irritation.
You caress my body with waves,
That soar to abode of memory.
Wide country, you are the one that defies poetic imagination.

My dears, you need to see the place,
To imagine its essence, and drink the cup of wide country.

'Bare feet' I stand on my yard, to think about my place, in the
scheme of things, so that I can uphold my stand as a right. I am
on the body of Mother Earth, the wide part of her body,
soothed by her breath. Kansas. I soak in this connection and
plot pots of poetry.

(Published in the *National Association of Women Writers' magazine*,
Sept. 2003).

Exile kills me with longing

Exile kills me with longing;
It squeezes, chokes, it slashes-

Exile clothes my body with memories:
Even the hated touts of Aba market,
Pull my heart with cords of longing.
But not so, for the khaki throne,
And guns that gaze at my midnight,
In this prison, this winter of my soul:

Fragments of Nine-Eleven

I do not understand this poem,
But its form stared vacuously at me,
Daring me to resist its alluring bait.
I dashed into my room for a pencil,
To capture this seductive picture.

But it laughed heartily,
Asking whether I picked poetry,
Like berries in watery curves of Maine.
The curves of Maine, I asked, trying to touch it,
To feel its contours and drink its essence.

Glass glazed the hand that dared to trap a spirit!
Blood and pain forced me to realize,
That it was the image of my body,
Naked in its original form,
That laughed at me through the bathroom mirror.

I picked the broken pieces,
Merged them with bloody elegance,
Like pieces of nine and eleven.
Can we put together, can we capture,
Can we remold, can we kill nine-eleven,
So that it never lived to hunt and hurt,
With bloody elegance that smears as it builds?

Fragments of nine-eleven,
Please, leave us in peace to bury the dead?

2.45 a.m., March 11, 2002

11

Bars Without Heart

I like these bars for they hear not,
The groans that keep vigil,
And wailing that announces the morn.

I love these bars, for they smell not,
The blood splashed across their faces,
And see not the hard visage of my jailer.

I loath these bars for they care naught,
That we kissed their blood-stained rods,
And sang the last prayer on their ears.

These bars.
Show me the navel of your wisdom,
That has no life so that I too can 'live'.

Robber at Large

The wall stares vacuously at me,
Longing for shelter in hollow spaces.

There is no respite,
For a wall reeking with cold,
And seeking dear heart,
Pocketed by a robber at large.

The wall trembles and drops a tear,
For vacant figure of its gaze.

At last...
I smile faintly,
... at the wall's empathy.

December 23, 1996

The Living Get Glued

I have seen so much adversity,
So much violence and tragedy,
That I am shocked to be touched,
By this red day.

I could not talk about it.
I did not want to watch it.

But I got glued to the screen.
The screen of Portland Hall,
Arrested me like a bullet.

The screen of Portland Hall,
Told tales more tragic than tragedy.
It told tales that defy poetic report,
Of lives lost in this new massacre.

It pulled up my tragic life,
From Biafra, and massacres,
To my dear ones gone beyond.

     I was alarmed!
     I stood up, wanting to escape.

     Then, I saw,
     I SAW THE LIVING GET GLUED
     IN TRAGEDIES YET TO COME!

     I made to run.

The wetness that coated my eyes,
Forced me to realize I was still glued,
As I kept watch at Portland Screen.

I want to talk, I want to shout.
I want to kill this image on my mind.
The image invoked by Portland screen.

11.30 p.m.: September 11, 2001
(Published in *Maine Progressive*, 2001)

Khakied Throne

His heart is a giant freezer,
Filled with cans of stolen goods,
And bottles snatched from mothers,
With flustered infants left at bay.

We shall storm the power house,
Cut supply of life,
From store house of ill-gotten goods.

War Mongers

Seven and seven times have passed.
The cycle of love and war runs over.
Drum draws the words of the goddess:

When I told you not to go there for firewood,
You cocked your ears like a swollen cocoyam,
Without care that ants dwell in the heart of the wood.
You went there where ants grow in the heart of wood!

You took my children to the wood with hidden ants.
You dislodged wood that grows ants in its navels.
Now ants scatter in the forest and scatter in my house.
Now my children scatter in the ant infested wood.

Do you think that I will let you go?
Do you think that I will not fight for mine?
Do you think that they will let you go?
You that poked the ant-infested wood.

You must think that I am a fool to lock ants in the wood.
You must think that you know more than your own mother.
Now confusion is on the high seat with disorderly mate,
You seek my face and proclaim a love that you know not.

There must be sacrifice for the confusion.
There must be sacrifice for the disorder.
But it shall not be my own children.

Memory

The arena is deserted.

Swept carcasses of fighters,
Dumped by circus owners.

The arena is deserted.

But,
The smell of blood!

Mashed souls,
Of my father's children,
Demand full funeral rites,
For clean resurrection.

Past and Present in a Waltz

The present holds hands with memory.
They litter my brain with fragments;
Images that come with battle.

"Don't cry,
Don't curse,
Come back to me,
Connect with me."

"Laugh, play, and ululate,
Don't try to stifle, cry a little."

"For my roses come with thorns,
Our dance must ride with fun and pain:"

News at Dawn

Neither table laden with goods,
Nor rare syrup from maple wood,
Awaiting hungry hands to ravage,
Could catch my fancy or soothe the damage,
Of my soul by news that came at dawn.

Tears find their doleful way,
Through dents and sores and bay,
Made by wreckage of my soul,
And cleavage of my hope and goal,
By news that came at dawn.

Where is my oasis,
In this doleful catharsis;
This play whose tragic part,
Has become my heart,
Since that news came at dawn?

Shall I look up to heaven,
With its promising coven,
Or wade in my own stream?
Shall I continue to scream,
And curse the news that came at dawn?

The breakfast table waits.
The plate shows its bait.
My angry hand fails to ravage,
Yet it cannot clear the damage,
Of the news that came at dawn.

March 30, 1996

Father

Shall I mourn,
For skin that smiles like the sun,
But has the coolness of the moon,
Or face that glows like fire,
But is harmless like a star?

It is not the plumes of the sun god,
Or his stunning exit from the arena,
It is,
This hollow sound echoing,
In my once complete soul,
That makes my heart to hurt.

October 1, 1987

Chains of Light

(for P. Ifeanyi)

The rosebud shows its face in doses.
Eyes roam bush and veld for roses.
Longing trails the sight of the veiled.
Eyes strive to lift curtain for the play.

Why does the smile leave my gate,
And tears unusual hours keep,
In corridors garnished with memory,
Across drapes, beyond veldts?

Shall I long for wind to lift the veil,
When I know that it never does?

I shall wait for the rosebud,
And its measured stingy doses.

July 29, 1996
(Published in *TurfWrite: A Creative Writing Journal*,
December 1999)

Counterattack

(for U. Monica)

Night has failed to starve indwelling pain.
Invading sunrays are deflected by ice,
That blocked this citadel of my being,
In its nomadic abode that attacks my soul.

Mockery's grating teeth wet my eyes.
The brain again does a quick addition,
My answer fails to prove the situation.

We shall call the teeth to order.
Assemble the calculating brains.
Weeping eyes will lead the team,

To free occupied soul from jail and pain.

Weep No More

Weep no more, dear heart,

For a star whose virtue,
Is same as saintly nature,
That surely leads as guide,
All saints are known to ride,
On their promised joyful way,
To the place we seek today.

Weep no more, dear heart,
For the sun will rise again.

My island shall smile anew,
With abundance from its rain,
When planted seeds and dew,
Shall merge and yield the vein,
That leads upwards with a smile.

Weep no more.

March 31, 1996
(After the memorial for P. Ifeanyi)

Who? (for Papa)

A gentle breeze passed,
Through earth in strides.

Mother borne through hills,
And mountains of our land.

He propped hungry fields,
And cut forests untouched.

He used the magic of the staff,
And the flower of his calling.

October 16, 1988

The Smile

The Ultimate has put a smile on my face.
I never knew that smile died on me,
Until now with this jump in my heart,
And the beams that caress my face;
Promises that defrost frozen dreams,
Of this smile that returned to my heart.

My hands cannot come down,
Nor my knees leave the ground,
That it kissed to make contact,
With Earth that joins the Sky.
I'll never cease to give my thanks.

July 5, 2006

It Has a Heart

It has a heart, after all.
It stops before its target.
It relents a while, allows me rest,
After all I have been through,
Thrashing and crying,
Twisting my torment.

It has a heart, after all, this inspiration pest.

- - -

But it does not rest.
I cannot sleep when it waits.
"Let us get on with it." I say.

"I'll adore you with scenes of love,
Of beauty that loves your heart."
"Let us get on with it." I say.

"Are you sure you don't mind," It grins,
Very glad that I oblige:

Always Near Like a Shield

S/He shields me
Like an umbrella wide and deep
Mother's wedge superior to iron and rock
Mightier than earth and sky and all I know
I know naught of the abode, the color and mode
I feel the presence all around my spaces, my world
Sound of guns I hear, but fail to see the caring Hand
That catches the bullets, halts guns and soothes my soul
I here thank the Leg that follows me all around, nice Hand
That shields me from harm, deep Eye that watches in my sleep
I know not any sloppy way to the high abode. I know the only one
I'll work my tireless way to the high dwelling to make my thanks
Thank You Dears for this prayer. This song that leaves my lay lips
I love Thee
My Mother
And Father
In Thy ways
That're dear
Try to hear
My lone cry
It does dry
This throat
That dreams
And yearns
Even though
You are there
Like a shield

The Sweetness in My Heart

Your love for me is a well that never dries.
Your love has no barricades for surtaxes,
Ceaselessly thrown at its abundant belly.

Your love for me is a river that never ebbs.
Your love scrubs my body with freshness,
My soul with laughter clothed in reverence.

Your love for me is a mirror of concern,
Facing savory contours and delicate scars,
Of this sweetness in my heart.

Firm my waist with Your arms,
So I may reach out and adore,
Your revered presence in my life.

Portrait of Love

Do you know ...... what I know?
Love is wayward....Love has no eyes
Eyes that see dents for it sees as it wants
Love has no sense of age, for no teenager
Or centurion can escapes the arrow of love
Love knows not gender or sex and cares not
For neither feminist nor malinistt escapes
That sting so sweet. Love moves by chance
Ties the unsuspecting, Laughs a while
Then it mocks the undeviating
Plants smiles on hearts
Some tears on eyes
This is love.

Goddess! Twin sister of Agwu,
And his brother Esu. I.know you
You respect not famine, plenty, or war
But arrest your targets in pain or mirth
Leaving them to tingle and tangle the rest.

You wayward goddess! Your tricks are well known
Yet victims still fall. We must plead with you
To see the ways of all Who divide with tribe
creed, age and all. Consider all these
When next you send your arrow.
I love you for not
Heeding this plea

Twin Kernel (for Tonebele)

She was little twinkle,
When I met her eyes,
Ocean eyes that smile.
The mouth also smiles,
Mouth colored with polite roses,
Roses without thorns on guard.

I prayed to the Ultimate Spirit,
"Protect this rose without thorns."

"How on earth did someone get at that mouth?"
This question, I throw at the One that protects.
"I allowed it. I am watching. Both are my children."

Remember this, surrogate thorn!
We all are watching!

But I am told that you are,
Like *akwu osukwu.*
You **too** are special. You **two** are special!

Touch My Heart

Can you hear my heart beating,
Like the little *ngagana* drum?
Can you see my soul breathing,
Like tom-tom arrested by flu?

Can't you see the wet eyes,
Talking of fever and storm,
Wrecking the comely capital,
And homestead of my soul?

Calm down my beloved.
I read the tone of your cry.
We shall go to the kraal,
To seek the healer herb.
There is music in the place,
To mend dented drum and tom-tom.

From Mother Heart

Can't you feel her breasts,
Like mounds of hot cassava,
Spitting heat and smoke?
Heat and smoke,
Ready to erupt,
In volcanic fire,
Before noontide!

Where in this homestead and beyond,
Lies the preying cockerel,
Whose crowing causes chaos?
Chaos and confusion,
In this furious heart!

I shall stir the waters,
And roam the rivers.
I shall go to God's house,
To bring cock and peace,
To my only child.

Kwaluseni Christmas

When the gun decrees a curfew,
The sun's drowsy eye is the cue,
And crow of timely cock the end.
Laughing day is left to dwell,
With loving Christmas spell,
And waltz the gala to its end.

Not so with Kwaluseni campus,
Where,
Silent monuments of white concrete,
Are testimonies of former occupants,
Of this bookish graveyard,
That has become our catacomb.

Excited cries of carousal from the veldt,
Distract silent ears of the Don that felt,
The grave-like silence has become her lot.
She skips and strikes a welcome poise,
For long imagined carol joys.

But yule-tide delight is not her lot.

At last she makes a bargain with silence,
Once faithful company, now a nuisance.
She girds her body in Swazi wrapper,
As she often has seen the women do.

Out of the grave, like a lancer,
She follows the sound of dancers.

Is That All?

Is that all,
In your sack?
Making figures that chew at me?

I must admit,
You have a heart indeed.

I'll ignore the past,
For this green sympathy,
Draws dreams of promises.

"I'll take you to the veldt,
To tales in moonlight.
I'll take you to the future,
To mountains of pride:"

Beauty That Knows Not Time

Streets of colors painted by the fall
World with one color made by the snow
Forests and crystals sculptured by ice
Watery presence punctuates the land
This is Portland.

Mbabane

A frolic,
Of gold and green,
Held up,
      To gods and djinn,
      By fingers,
      Proud mountains,
      Clasped,
      In smug embrace.

Manzini from the Air

Mounds of earth's crust,
Like smiling breasts,
Of *umhlanga* maidens,
Doing nuptial dance.

Mounds of earth's crust,
Like wriggling streams,
Making lazy way,
In haste to the sea,

Mounds of earth's crust,
Salute these eyes,
Making maiden entry,
To the city of Manzini.

Mounds of earth's crust!
Armed guards of Swazi soil!

Like walls of Benin,
You form a barricade,
Around Manzini!

Autumn Colours

Bros, Can you smell the mild shades of autumn,
Spread out like a festival of departing masks,
In these wild ridges of Ithaca New York?

His protest is furious:

"Brown ghost, blue ghost,
Amber-like ghost of dying flakes;
They whimper and carpet green fields!
Even dying greenish leaves."

He fumes without break:

"There are no black leaves,
To add color to this wood of withering world.
No leaves bend to the wind's caress,
With courtesies and bows,
As flakes scatter in the wood!"

Not so, my father's son,
I feel the beauty of the-
"Cancer stricken and suffering wood?" He snaps.

I feel its glorious death in the-
"Cancerous shades that lead to Hades?"

You see sHades as dangerous,
But sHades is illustrious,
Termination of cyclic mutation.

Manzini Homestead

Like a bazaar of egrets,
In cocoons of green trees -
Avo-ca-do, man-go,
Paw-paw and Pump-kin -
Manzini homesteads rest,
In the bowls of lusty hills.

Hills clasp hands,
Like arms of warriors,
Ready for encounter,
At the king's bidding.

The hands rise with bounties,
For homesteads and counties,
In the bowls of lusty hills.

Forests of Guava

Green hills, you get darker,
As eyes journey from the hills,
Counting the hills of guava,
That garnish Swazi veldt.

Thank you Lord for the hills,
And their hairs of guava trees.
Thank you Lord for the trees,
And their heads of guava fruit.

Thank you Lord for the fruit,
And their juicy tasty flesh.
Thank you Lord for tasty flesh,
That feeds birds and all of us.

I thank you for the wild birds,
That send seeds to the hills,
That give birth to guava trees,
That feed the hills of our land.

(Published in *Yebo Weekend Observer*, January 18, 1997)

Eyes of One Love

"Poor kid, Dear buddy, suffering alone,
In Africa there, without romance.
No candle-light dinner, and 'love you darling,"
Mouthed anew,
In lonesome abode,
Of exotic hotel,
Standing erect,
In toxic allure.

Not so, dear Eye, west of the sea.
Not so, dear lady, come close and see,
Eye of the woman east of the sea.

How she ranted and raved,
For murdered izorah,
Given with words,
Smelling of love,
Hotter than fire,
of Harmattan night.

"Di man dey craze!"
She shouted in rage,
Mocking the ways,
Of the Izorah man.

"He knows no thing,
Of African romance:
How dem wink and tease.
How dem woo my mother,
And work for our farm.
Dress up for dance,
Jazz in moon-light.

Spray me with gifts,
Of coral and coins,
Not murdered Izorah,
Bleeding like death."

Lady Eye says from over the sea,

"Poor kid. Dear buddy, suffering so long,
In Africa there, without a thrill,
Of tonic or twirl to pep up the chest."

Not so, dear buddy, from over the sea.
Not so, dear lady, come close and see,
The woman, your friend.

She cackles her eyes,
At the cushions in bags,
Procured with words,
That tickles her nose,
And gives her the dread.

"You know not the size,
The make of the land,
That factory my chest,
For all of our kids,
In wait like the gem.

Thank you dear lady, your thought, your love."

Still It Lashes

Still it trashes and lashes,
From seven to seven,
It will not give me time,
To pause or time to rest.

I admit,
That the dance is gorgeous,
But tortuous indeed.

"You should be happy, with pots that you win!"
It says and pats my back, not breaking the ride.
It does not mind that they're born in pain.
It does not care that I want to rest.
Oh, the wicked spirit!
Dishing and slashing:

Globalization

What does this Globalization mean?
It is a new thing that has descended.
It crossed seven seas and seven times,
And landed with grammar of its own.
It is called Gbalaganoze.

It is a puzzle with many holes many sides.
On my side, it is a disease without name.
Yaws that shine with oil clothed in shame.
So we marshal our gallant herbal juices,
To chase out Globalization.

But they cannot recognize its face,
Because it masks its yaws with regalia.
It's like cancer in the garb of malaria.
Our malaria warriors see its tricks,
And shout to us, Gbalaganoze-o!

We run to the bush for that is Gbalaganoze,
But the bush is no sanctuary from its gas.
For even our air is polluted with its fart.
We cannot embrace the sea and feed of its fish,
For the water is poisoned with its excrement.
Belly-ache is our new song of puzzlement,
Since our food is infected with this new thing.

Gbalaga-na-oze means 'take refuge in the land,'
But my child who read book says another thing.
For my child Gbalaganoze means 'run from the land.'
My child says that globalization is good for you.

BUT

I hold my belly and stand on the body of my land.
There is healing here from the bowel of my Earth,
In this fight with the unknown thing that is called
Globalization.

The Refugee

I saw the woman in a refugee camp,
Her eyes wacky like congealed blood.
Tales of carnage, like angry tornadoes,
Spilled tragedies that lodge in my heart.

Tales of villages turned to deserts,
Garnished with skeletons of her folks,
As relics of once human habitation.

In spite of the tales and because of the tales,
Hope lives in the eyes of the woman,
In the silent conference within herself,
And promises of the scars on her body.

Hope still lives in the eyes of the woman,
And sends spikes of hope to all of our hearts,
In garbs of tragedy that seek compassion.

Hope lives in the eyes of the woman,
That builds the fort of expectation,
In tales that demand all attention.

When I Get Your Heart

Green mamba!
You swallowed my child,
While my body shriveled,
In Island of sorrow.

So ugly shall I make you that even maggots will not eat,
And generations will forever spit at your remains for:

I shall get your heart.
I shall place your heart on a golden tray,
For all to see your heart.
Slowly, I shall carve your heart,
Into two point eight billion bits.

January 13, 1997
(Coming from Robben Island)

Umsenge Tree

They tell me you are beautiful,
That you are easy and fanciful.

I think you are pitiful.
You're snooty and stout,
With fang-like fingers,
Ready to pounce and tear.

They tell me you are useful,
Shelter those that are dutiful.

I think you are devious.
You house *sahuulal*, the owl,
To assault the ear with sound.
You are a wicked war cry.

I shall never go alone,
Never to the river dome,
Where you hide to jeer,
At souls that come near,
Your horrid hunted home.

(Published in *Yebo Weekend Observer*, January 18, 1997

Christmas Train

Christmas,
Streets of masks, romping and running with playful people.
Christmas,
Crowds of followers, feasting and frolicking, old friends and all.
Christmas,
Pilgrimage to ancestral home, where old ones keep hearth alive.
Christmas,
Display of arrogance by exotic cars from Tokyo and Taiwan,
Vying to slay the local and tired, in battered old trucks.

Christmas,
You are extra awareness of apart hood.

In exile,
You are a strain murmured alone.

Johannesburg

Carnival of stars.
Festival of saints.

Medieval confusion,
Seasoned in division.

You are a massive meal,
Grilled and garnished,
By treasures and weeds.

Let the bait of love not deceive thee,
Or the song of memory confound thee.
May you hold the monkey and spider all in one.

When Brain Is the Color of Blood

When blood usurps grey-matter,
Anarchy wears a purple garb,
Commands the army of locusts,
Slashing and barking "so be it."

When blood sits on the brain,
And makes rules for the world,
Tragedy makes a new creed,
For slashers barking "serve 'em right."

See the color of our grey-matter!
It's just the same color of blood,
That powers the brain of slashers.
The mirror of our tragic heart.

We slash with our silence.
We slash with our speeches.
The arrogant voice that talks,
About the Huttus and Tutsis,
When brain is the color of blood.

A Dance of Love

Even a dance of love,
Needs a pause, time to recess,
Relish desire and all the rest,
That come from heat and zeal of ball.

But the muse, my allied twin,
Has no heart to feel my thirst,
To savor dishes of our dance.

It prances and brags.
Of brand new scenes:

Happiness

Happiness is:
Waking up and opening eyes that see.
It is drinking the air of satisfaction.
It is stretching dreamy hands and legs.
It is yawning my mouth to wakefulness.

Happiness is:
Remembering loved ones far and near.
It is memories that whisper in the ear.
It is scenes of survival and triumph.
It is dreams that assuage my heart.

Happiness is:
Getting a cup to wake the veins.
The work ahead without regret.
It is music that caresses the soul.
It is the sun massaging my body.

Happiness knows that I am here.
Happiness is the world and I.
It is recollection, it is my soul,
Happiness is here, Happiness is now.

Mother Speaks I Am

(for Michael and Chinedu)

To be a man is:
To affirm in me and my action,
"I am very tall very huge,
In my guts, my heart, my spirit."

To be a man is:
To affirm to me, in my action,
"I rise up to the occasion,
With best of my ability."

To be a man is:
To affirm in me, with my action,
"I know who I am,
I love who I am,
I respect that in me,
I also respect others."

To be a man is:
"To still be my mother's child,
The child of my dad, my land,
And my Maker,
Even as I rise to higher grounds,
In my goal, new family, and me."

7:30 a.m., January 8, 2006.

Daughters of Earth

(for Kelechi and Chinyerugo)

Like the unfolding of a flower,
Burnishing of common metal,
That becomes the prized silver,
So is progress to womanhood.

Like the journey of the sun,
With sweet, sweat and heat,
So is your courage,
As you take your first steps,
In the process of becoming.

The moon in a world that is dark,
Knows who she is; she affirms self,
And becomes the light in the dark.
So is your strength as you waltz through,
Your journey to higher grounds.

Assert Ani on which you stand.
The umbilical chord is testimony,
Of your coming and bond with the land,
That saw the dance of your beginnings.

All your fathers and mothers join,
And pray the Ultimate to hold you,
To guide your journey in all places.
We sing unending chorus of "so be it."

Di

Shades of straight and kinky hairs,
Join in waltz of love and grief,
For burnt-out candle of the Isle.

A silent shout at paparazzi,
That lent a hand to marauder,
Vicious in seizing of the heart,
And her tanned attendant knight.

We crave for more candles,
To quench the fire of bias,
More potent than paparazzi,
Fire that escapes the marauder.

No Matter What Happens

(for Women & Men In Need)

No matter what people think or say about me,
No matter what I did or failed to do in life,
No matter the circumstances I find myself in,
No matter what happened or might happen to me,
No matter how far I fall and how deep I hurt,
No matter how much I cry and how much I curse,
No matter how painted by strife dented by smear;

I am still who I am, still loved by God, still loved by Me.

I hold on to my self my spirit and my God.
I hold on to any, who still believes in me,
Anyone who still loves me for who I am,
Anyone who knows that the tide will rise!

The one that knows might be just me, for I believe in Me.

12.30 p.m., April 3, 2003

Yes

(for M. Shalom)

Yes!
Eyes,
On the goal,
Ears filter dirt,
Burden on the bag,
And joy on forehead,
As you glide and bump,
Through this labyrinthine.

Laughter

Sun of the smith's face!
Moon of feverish lips,
Of anxious customers!
Breasts skip in their bags,
Glittering eyes wet with joy,
Because,
Like gun-shot,
You arrest the soul,
Causing fiery burst,
Of joyful cries,
To break through dormant teeth!

Laughter,
Wild child of my land,
Sweet song of my heart,
Clad in white cloth.
With pearls of joy,
You dazzle the eyes,
Causing stick-scrubbed teeth,
To dazzle and lure,
Attract and seize,
For you are heartily infectious.

Published in *From Earth's Bedchanber*, 1966

Harmony in Song

Yes indeed,
The dance is sweet.
Its smell, its shade,
Even the curves and dents,
That garnish the pots,
Spread out in summer bloom,
For all to see and hail;

All are harmony in song.

Waiting is grief,
For dance is bliss.
Let the ball move.
We need to bask.

I sing its song,
Dance its dance.
It brags of more:

Sire That Yells

One nation, scattered.
        Many wives, one man with one goal.
         So many...wives...and kids,
            some thin,
    Some big, some glorious, and lascivious.
They fight with fire!
And tear the sire!
They do not tire!
In battle dire!
This plentiful family, like pieces of gourd,
And fighting zones, alliances that form,
        And deform,
...till death the sire does a ghostly turn.
Time for union in burial and truce to share the filial cake.
            Dawn of new
            plots! And
            battles foul!
Yes indeed!

(Published in *Englishes*, Vol.10, 2000)

One Nation

One tree
Many limbs and leaves
Some green, zestful and peaceful
Some yellow brown nestled on the stem
Some adored and loved but hated by some
They quest for light and space. They touch
They kiss. They love and laugh in one tree
One mother, one stem, and many children
Swelling, flowering, and then fruiting
Smiling and feeding locusts of mouths
Sweet mother of this dear land
One nation with many parts.
This our solid base
In a mighty maze
One tough head
Our own knight
Several riddles
Solve them right
Headaches cure
And flames fight
In this dear body
That holds on tight
Hugs this same place
This tree, that has might
This haven that echoes hell
This Iroko tree that is so swell
Needs its parts to end this knell
My grand child yet unborn will smile
Her mother yet unborn will like to retell
Of once scattered house of sire that yelled
August 17, 1994 (Riots, broadcasts, and talks of disintegration and division)

(Published in *Englishes* Vol. 10.4, 2000)

Earth and Sky

May Earth
Receive wakeful rays
That are forceful and gay
As they reward friendly fine fingers
Of this beloved earthen acolyte, molding
Sniffing and Stroking, swinging and wielding
Fresh sweetness fond of circles of lusciousness:
Oneness of earth and sky spread like pots of poetry
Like birds basking in sunny greenness and rainbow
Our Sweet Mother that sweats for us far and near
Dear Earth, sweet and vast and so very dear
Do not send a burning rage on erring kids
That spoil our soil and try to strangle
Others who do not tangle or plunder
Allow not Sky, your allied Mate
And He that made all and fate
Send down fire or thunder
Swift and sharp.
We need time to revamp and rebuild mounds soaked in pools of dirt.
And time to design new ones, fresher ones to embellish earth and sky.

(Inspired by "Pots," a painting by Nneka Obiora, August 1993)

When We Wake Is Our Morn

When we wake is our morning.
And when we sleep is our night.
When we stop is the seven.
Seven seas mark the end.
Three times mark the end.
And the hill can be the end.

So it's time for the first pot.
"Your maiden pot when you were a girl."
"Your very first poem."

"My very first poem":

My Very First Poem (For Edwin O)

It was for you that I wrote my very first poem,
That sketched your smile, and your broken leg,
Just as you showed it to me on that red day.

It was your silence at that last meeting,
When my childish heart asked you the question,
That congealed the tears within my eyes.

All my life I waited for you to give me a reply,
For my eyes could not decode the sign of your smile.
Now the centurion of this life has come to my aid,
And taught me to know that your smile is iced up forever.

Only now have I shed the long awaited tear,
That hung on my eyes like congealed blood.
It's not too late to shed tears for you my dear,
It's not late to put a lid on the pot of hope.

Your silent smile, the gift you left for me,
Has grown in my heart as stunning as you,
And links its arms of comfort with me.
Your memory is truly a gift from God.

One last memo though you won't reply.
It hurts a little to know you're so happy,
That you never say hello to those of us here.

You're so happy and content in your world.

I'm happy; your memory lives in my heart.

Unsung Soldiers

It is not clear why you compel me,
To remember the unsung soldiers,
The innocents who knew not the full picture,
And plunged with zeal of love for their land.

They also are victims you say.

They also are victims, I agree,
That they are heroes still,
They hurt and bled like all of us.
They loved, were loved, and still loved.

Seven at Last

At last, it is seven by its own devise,
For this is the time of final descent,
And blissful relish,
The painful joy of all that we did.

But why all the pain,
In a thing so good?

A spell takes over,
The need for answer:

Why Winter?

Igbo	Translation
Ujiri di uto,	Apple that is sweet,
Na anyi ido.	Frolics with soldier ants.

I jump from the maze,
As I wake with a frown:

"Why should this head,
Go through the thorn?"

This query I threw at God,
With a frown on my face.

Contemplation wraps my brain,
As I spring up with a frown.

I love the wholesome apple fruit,
But I never swing its lofty tree,
For pests assail its lasting limbs.

We threw our sticks from afar,
With hope to knock down fruit,
From the pretty apple tree.

Did they ever land intact?
Untouched by the fighting ants?

It's true;
Happy does live with pains.

The Truth

Yes indeed:
No summer without winter.
For winter is pregnant.

To tell you the truth,
I did enjoy,
M-most of it.
"Let's do IT again."

Already it snores.

Alone at Last

Through joyful dance and playful pranks,
I received seven-headed pack with thanks.

In painful phase of nine moon's waiting,
Without my muse, I labored with fainting.

I recall the promise of the dating,
Including assurance of the petting.

The moon has departed.
Its place is deserted.
Copies of promises,
Reign its premises.

The prize kicking and lashing like the donor,
Recalls that dance of seven without honor.
Alone in labor ward without a word,
From gallant dancer, seven o'clock lord.

I wrap my gift on paper and pen,
For baby show proposed at noon.

Amazing Twin

Unexpected, it appears.
Uninvited, it replies,
Watchful and keen,
Its presence alluring,
Its essence compelling,
My attention and intent.

"What is it?" I say.
"I salute you."
"What is it you want?"

"I still love you."
"So what?" I snap.

"Love me again."
"Please." It adds.

Its eye recedes,
Like a watchful cat, eager to pounce,
At the least sign from this ready prey,
Softening again for another dance.

The Waiting

(For all of us who do nothing about the chaos in the world –
wars, genocides, exploitation and other despoliations of Mother
Earth).

From different sectors of my body,
Greeders make war on me:

They poke my nose and dig my bowels,
Expose my sweet and secret places,
With sacraments of their greediness!

They unmask my sacred places.
They dig the hills and valleys of my body,
And make excuses for their greed.

- - -

Chaos holds summit unquestioned by sense.
Heat climbs the mountain untouched by rain.
The rock explodes in two point eight billion bits.
And Earth thunders and thunders and thunders!

Silence ...

Silence ...

Silence ...

- - -

Silence

- - -

There is silence in the world.

The silent ones wait.
We listen to the sound of lions.
The sound of royal tricksters.
Yet, we hear nothing in our silence.

We hear nothing,
For we are too numbed, too afraid of this life that we are not living,
We want to live long but we are not living life.
We say nothing.

We say nothing,
For we are too numbed, too afraid of this life that we are not living,
We want to live long but we are not living life.
We do nothing.

Yes, we toil.
We cry in our silences.
Too numbed, too afraid of this life that we are not living,
We want to live long but we are not living life.

Waiting ….

As silent mourners at graveyards,
Of coming demise of our bodies,
Backed to the abyss by the lions,
That we can see, that we can stop,
In our silence.

We take our power,
To the grave.

OR

We take our power,
To live life.

Glossary

Aba Market. Aba is a city in the southeastern part of Igboland, Nigeria. It is famous for its extensive outdoor market that is a center for regional, national, and international trade. On the artistic level, impromptu theatrical happenings are common and both buyers and sellers readily constitute participating audience. The commonest performers of impromptu spectacles are the touts. Whether they are cajoling passengers to go for a particular bus, engaging in a pretend-fight, or taking on a woman in mini skirt, they usually attract other people who get involved in the action by taking sides in the 'conflict,' admonishing or supporting them, as the fun goes on.

Agwu. Igbo spirit of creativity and confusion.

Akwu-osukwu. Akwu is the juicy palm fruit. It is very useful because every item in it is raw material for products such as *mmanu* (cooking oil), *egbendulu* (candle), and *ude-aki* (body lotion). Its kernel is snack and the seed-shells make good fuel. *Akwu-osukwu* is a rare variety of *akwu* noted for its succulence, high quality red juice, and little or no hard seeds.

Ani. The Igbo spirit of the earth (goddess) is known for wealth, power, peace, and reproach. *Ona-ocha* (silver) is her prominent apparatus although *ona-edo* (gold), *nzu* (chalk), and *kalari* (coral) are also present. Everything is linked to Mother Earth.

Aro-of-God. Aro is a sub-Igbo group dispersed in various states as towns, clans, villages, and lineages whose original homeland is in Arochukwu. "Chi" translates as "spirit", "ukwu" translates as big, and "Chi-Ukwu" translates as Big-Spirit (God), so Arochukwu is a compound name rendered here as "Aro people of God." In pre-colonial times, Arochukwu was noted for her oracle called Chukwu-Ibini Ukpabi. Aro elite formed oracular and trade links to various places where they were referred to as "umu-Chukwu" (children of God) because of their oracle and oracular activities.

Benin. Capital of Edo State, Nigeria; known for its long history and old traditions that are evident in visible symbols like the walls of the 15th century Benin-city, Oba's palace, and bronze works.

Biafra. Located on the southeastern part of the Atlantic coast of Nigeria by the bight of Biafra, she was at war with Nigeria from 1967 to 1970. The State was of brief existence, but is historically significant.

Bitterleaf. Called *onugbo* in Igbo (Nigeria), this vegetable is very bitter, but a very popular delicacy when properly washed and used in soups. It is also known for its medicinal qualities.

Esu. Yoruba spirit of confusion and creativity.

Gbalaganoze (*gbala ga na oze*). Run to the bush

Guava. Tropical tree about fifteen feet height that makes abundant round or oval fruits that are yellowish when ripe. Also called guyava, kuawa.

Harmattan. West African season—chilly, dry, windy; usually from December to January.

How dem... From Nigerian pigeon language, "dem" translates as "they."

Hutus and Tutsis. Hutu and Tutsi are the names of two economic classes with the same language and traditions in Burundi and Rwanda. Favored by the colonizers, Germans and later Belgians, who distinguished the groups by occupation and the number of cattle they owned, the Tutsis got more education, wealth, and political power in the colonial state. Angered by colonial favoritism, the non-favored or Hutus who were largely farmers and peasants resented their exclusion. The Tutsis also guarded their power and position. Complications from the resentments and suspicions as well as political power changes that occurred after the Belgians left generated sub-ethnic cleansing that took the lives of millions for almost a decade while the international powers and We watched.

Hun jin. A kind of *Tae Kwon Do* punch.

Izorah. A tropical flower, commonly red or purple.

Kwaluseni. A small town in Swaziland whose main importance lies in its being the site of the main campus of the University of Swaziland.

Mamba. A fast-moving snake known in Southern African region for the high toxicity of its venom. It is dangerous, poisonous, deadly, feared and hated.

Mbabane. Capital of Swaziland, situated on hills in the high veldt area of the country.

Manzini. A city in Swaziland.

Nsukka. A major center of artistic creativity in southeastern Nigeria, and home of The University of Nigeria. As a young girl, the hills of Nsukka used to amaze me with their chain that appeared to be linking hands. A set of hills that I perceived as triplets were my favorites because they appeared magical - "moving" from one side of the road to the other.

Ngagana. Swazi name for drum.

Portland Hall. Residential Hall of the University of Southern Maine, Portland, ME.

Robben Island. An island on the coast of South Africa. It is naturally the home of penguins, but notorious during the apartheid period for its prison that housed political prisoners including Nelson Mandela, the first president of democratic South Africa.

Sahuulal. Swazi name for owl.

Swaz. Short for Swaziland.

77

Tae Kwon Do. Martial art of Korean origin that relies on the science of kicking and punching. In Korea, *tae* means "to kick", *kwon* means "to punch" and *do* means "method," hence the composite noun "Tae Kwon do."

Twin-Kernel. Kernel is the seed of palm nut. It is rare to find a nut that has two seeds, which are like twins, but it exists and is special.

Umhlanga. An annual festival of rejuvenation in which women march from all sectors of Swaziland to the capital where they perform ceremonial dances in honor of womanhood and society. In colorful costumes that show their bodies to advantage, girls perform the ritualized dance movements before the public and the iNdlovukazi (Queen Mother) whose son, the Ngweyama (king), also joins the men's regiment whose dance complements that of the women and children.

Umsenge Tree. Outstanding in the veldt for it is relatively tall with groves and stumps that make it appear creepy.

Chronology of Author's life

2005 – Birth of Chinyerugo and Chinedu.
2004 – Global Learning Most Outstanding Department Award
2003 – Associate Professor, Wichita State University, Wichita, Kansas.
2001– Associate Professor, University of Southern Maine, Portland ME.
1998 – Writer-In-Residence, Rockefeller Center, Bellagio, Italy.
1996 – Senior Lecturer and Coordinator of Literature, Univ. of Swaziland.
1996 – Outstanding Finalist, The Bertram's V. O. Literature of Africa Awards; South Africa.
1994 – Special Discovery of the Association of Nigerian Authors (ANA) 1994, for proficiency as a Writer in the three genres of literature - poetry, prose and drama.
1994 – 2nd Place, Association of Nigerian Authors' (ANA) National Competition for Prose.
1994 – Honors, Association of Nigerian Authors' (ANA) National Competition for Poetry.
1994 – 4th Place, Association of Nigerian Authors' (ANA) National Competition for playwriting.
1994 – Associate Professor, University of Benin. Nigeria.
1992 – 3rd Prize, Short Story Competition. Women's Research and Documentation Center (WORDOC), University of Ibadan, Nigeria.
1992 – Postdoctoral Research Fellow, Cornell University, Ithaca, New York
1991 – Rockefeller Award, Hunter College, State University of New York.
1989 – Ph.D. English, University of Nigeria, Nsukka. Nigeria
1980 – Lecturer II - University of Benin. Nigeria.
1979 – M.A. African Studies, University of Sussex, Brighton, U.K.

1978 –	Assistant lecturer, University of Port-Harcourt. Nigeria.
1977 –	Pg.D. Theatre Studies, University College, Cardiff. U.K.
1975 –	B.A. English, University of Nigeria, Nsukka.
1971–	Graduated from High School, Queen's School, Enugu, Nigeria.
1969–	Attended Government Emergency Secondary School, Akokwa, Biafra.
1965 –	Attended Rosary High School, Awgu, Nigeria.